Who Was
Ferdinand
Magellan?

FERDINAND MAGELLAN

Who Was Ferdinand Magellan?

By Sydelle Kramer

Illustrated by Elizabeth Wolf

Grosset & Dunlap • New York

To Hopey, who's been
around the world too—S.K.

For Bill—E.W.

Text copyright © 2004 by Sydelle Kramer. Illustrations copyright © 2004 by Elizabeth Wolf. Cover illustration © 2004 by Nancy Harrison. All rights reserved. Published by Grosset & Dunlap, a division of Penguin Young Readers Group, 345 Hudson Street, New York, New York 10014. GROSSET & DUNLAP is a trademark of Penguin Group (USA) Inc. Printed in the U.S.A.

Library of Congress Cataloging-in-Publication Data

Kramer, Sydelle.
  Who was Ferdinand Magellan? / by Sydelle Kramer ; illustrated by Elizabeth Wolf.
    v. cm.
  Contents: Who was Ferdinand Magellan? — The boy becomes a man — War hero — A new king listens — Getting ready — Tricky seas — Frozen in — The Pacific — The crossing — The last battle — End of the journey.
  ISBN 0-448-43356-7 — ISBN 0-448-43105-X (pbk.)
  1. Magalhäaes, Fernäao de, d. 1521—Juvenile literature. 2. Explorers—Portugal—Biography—Juvenile literature. 3. Voyages around the world—Juvenile literature. [1. Magellan, Ferdinand, d. 1521 2. Explorers. 3. Voyages around the world.] I. Wolf, Elizabeth, 1954– ill. II. Title.
  G286.M2K76 2004
  910'.92—dc22

                              2003021264

ISBN 0-448-43105-X (pbk)   10 9 8 7 6 5 4 3 2 1
ISBN 0-448-43356-7 (GB)   10 9 8 7 6 5 4 3 2 1

Contents

Who Was
Ferdinand Magellan?

Imagine a time when no one was sure the Earth was round . . . when people believed they'd topple over the edge if they sailed too far from home. Imagine a time when most people didn't know there was a Pacific Ocean. Go back five hundred years, when whole continents were still undiscovered, when people thought the Earth was tiny and that monsters swam through its waters. Yet one man decided to sail his ship through unknown seas and discover what was out there.

He was not the first to make such a perilous voyage. But he went farther and stayed away longer than anyone had before. Because of his brains and courage, he is known for being the first man to circumnavigate—sail around—the globe.

Who was he?

Ferdinand Magellan.

Magellan

Chapter 1
The Boy Becomes a Man

Sometime around 1480 in Portugal, a boy named Ferdinand was born to the Magellan family. The Magellans were of noble blood, but they had little money or power. They owned a farm far from the sea. This was where Ferdinand, the youngest of

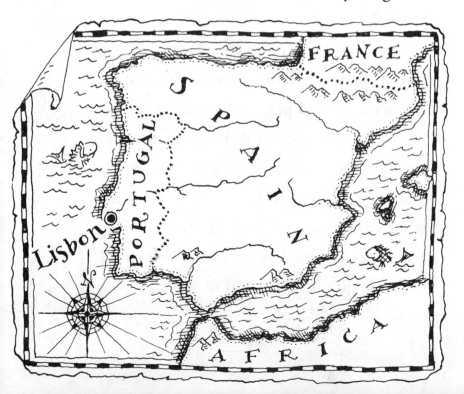

three children, grew up. Their house wasn't fancy: The family lived on the top floor and their cows, goats, sheep, and chickens lived on the bottom.

Ferdinand's life changed around the time he turned twelve. Portugal's queen, Leonora, needed pages. Pages were boys who ran messages and did errands for the royal family. Ferdinand was chosen for the job. Pages didn't just work. They received a good education and met the most important people in the land. A clever boy could make the job his first step to success.

Page

So Ferdinand left home for Lisbon, the capital of Portugal. The lad who had never seen the ocean found himself in a city right on the coast. What a place it was! Lisbon's harbor was crammed with graceful sailing ships, and its docks overflowed with goods from faraway ports. There was gold and there was silk. And there were spices—pepper, cloves, ginger, nutmeg, and cinnamon. Spices were valuable because they were used to make beer. They also made meat and other foods taste better. Most important of all, though, they kept food from spoiling.

Spices were very expensive. That's because most of them came from Asia, thousands of miles from Portugal. Spices grew in countries like India and in those we now call Sri Lanka

Pepper

Ginger

Cloves

Cinnamon

Nutmeg

and Indonesia. The Moluccas, or Spice Islands, part of Indonesia, were the richest of all. But

traveling from Europe to these islands was difficult and dangerous.

In Ferdinand's day, the only way to bring back these spices from far-off places was to take the Spice Route. This was a long path over both land

and sea, winding through Asia, where the spices grew, across the Indian Ocean, through the Middle East, and on to the city of Venice.

For eight hundred years, Arabs had control of the Spice Route. Together with their trading partners in Venice, they sold the precious goods for high prices.

But what if a country found a new route to Asia? Then it could get spices on its own. It could make a fortune. The new route had to be by sea alone. That was the only way to avoid Arab lands.

The Portuguese wanted to take over the spice trade. So they built a powerful navy. From the mid-1400s, they had been sending ships to search for a direct sea route to Asia.

Spain sought the very same route. It had a strong navy too. In 1492 just about the time Ferdinand became a page, Spain's king and queen sent Christopher Columbus across the

Christopher Columbus

Atlantic to find Asia. Instead, he stumbled onto
North America.

Columbus's Ships

Santa Maria   Pinta   Nina

By 1494, the competition between Portugal and
Spain was so fierce that they almost went to war.
But the two countries agreed to divide the world in
half. A line was drawn down the middle of a map.
Spain could claim all lands to the west of the line.
Portugal could claim all lands to the east. The two
countries also agreed never to sail through the
other's territory.

It was probably around this time that young
Ferdinand Magellan decided to become an explorer.
After all, the queen of Portugal's palace was close to

the harbor, and he could watch the beautiful ships come and go. At the palace, there was constant talk about the great sea captains and the riches and fame earned from spices. After his father and mother died, Ferdinand had no reason to return to his hometown. He placed his faith in God and believed his destiny was to go to sea.

PORTUGAL and SPAIN

WHO PREVENTED WAR BETWEEN PORTUGAL AND SPAIN IN 1494? THE POPE, ALEXANDER VI. THE POPE HAD THAT MUCH POWER BECAUSE BOTH PORTUGAL AND SPAIN WERE RULED BY CATHOLIC KINGS. SO, WHEN HE CAME UP WITH A WAY TO SETTLE THEIR FIGHT, THEY DIDN'T REFUSE. HE GAVE SPAIN ONE HALF OF THE WORLD AND PORTUGAL THE OTHER.

Pope Alexander VI

By 1496, sixteen-year-old Ferdinand was a government clerk. He helped set up voyages to Asia for great captains like Vasco da Gama. It was da Gama who, in 1498, made the great discovery of a sea route to India. Now, Portugal no longer needed to trade with the Arabs. It could buy spices on its own. Vasco da Gama became a national hero, and Portugal began building forts and trading posts on the African and Indian coasts.

If only Ferdinand could sail to Asia. Ships were leaving constantly with hundreds of young sailors onboard. But Ferdinand couldn't convince anyone to let him go. He did his job well. However, he didn't know the right people. Powerful people. To make things worse, the new king of Portugal, Manuel, disliked him. No historians know why, but some guess that the king was a snob and thought the teenaged Ferdinand was a country bumpkin.

Manuel couldn't see that Ferdinand had a steely will and a strong heart. Not even a king could stop him.

the AGE of EXPLORATION

IN 1416 A GREAT PRINCE OF PORTUGAL NAMED HENRY THE NAVIGATOR ENCOURAGED CAPTAINS TO FIND NEW COUNTRIES AND LEARN ABOUT THE WORLD. HE WANTED PORTUGAL TO RULE THESE NEW LANDS AND BECOME THE WORLD'S GREATEST POWER.

PORTUGUESE EXPLORERS FIRST SAILED SOUTH THROUGH THE ATLANTIC AND REACHED THE WEST COAST OF AFRICA. THEN IN 1488, WHEN FERDINAND MAGELLAN WAS STILL IN SCHOOL, BARTOLOMEU DIAS SAILED AROUND THE TIP OF AFRICA. THE NEXT STEP WAS TO SAIL ALL THE WAY TO ASIA. THE AGE OF EXPLORATION HAD BEGUN. VASCO DA GAMA REACHED INDIA IN 1498.

Prince Henry the Navigator

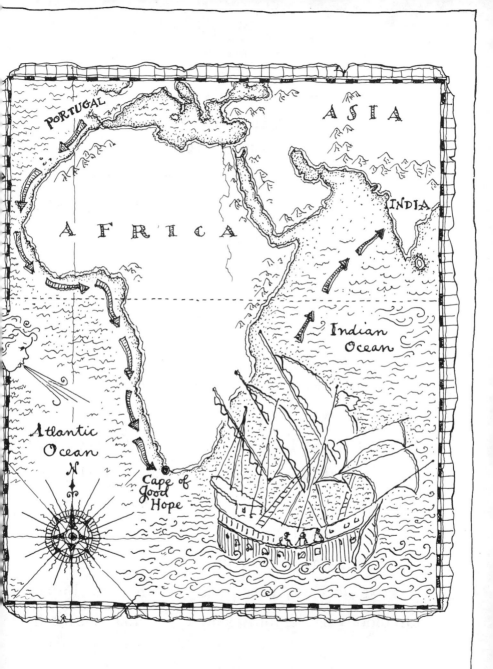

Chapter 2
War Hero

The Portuguese soon discovered that the Arabs were not about to give up their spice trade without a fight. By 1505, the Arab navy attacked Portugal's ships. King Manuel struck back. He ordered his fleet to take control of sea routes across the Indian Ocean.

Portugal was going to war. And Ferdinand decided he was going to be part of it. He wouldn't be paid a penny for risking his life. Still, becoming a soldier was his chance to get away. His religious faith had always been strong, and now he believed his God would protect him. Plus, with luck, he'd make a fortune, and a name for himself.

First stop was East Africa. Then came India. On bloody battlegrounds there, Ferdinand learned to be a fearless and brutal soldier. Though he was short, he was tough and strong and quick-witted. He had such trust in his own instincts that it never occurred to him to doubt himself. He was a natural leader.

By 1509, Ferdinand had become a lieutenant. Then, in a battle on the Indian coast, he was wounded so badly that he was in a hospital for close to five months. His reward was twenty sacks of wheat. It wasn't much, but Ferdinand didn't mind. He went back to sea as soon as he recovered. He boldly rescued sailors trapped by the enemy and captured Chinese pirates. For his heroism, he was promoted to captain.

By 1513, Ferdinand was back in Lisbon. Despite his military feats, he was as poor as when he'd left,

and almost as unknown. He found a city buzzing with business, full of wealthy men. Ferdinand had nothing. Except his dream.

Now thirty-three years old, he wanted to be the captain on a ship bound for Asia. He was certain he could find a fast route there. But he needed someone rich to buy him a ship. And no one would.

He couldn't understand why. Here he was, a man with courage and confidence, a proven leader. He had a feel for the sea, the wind, and the stars. He was a great navigator. Why wouldn't anyone give him a chance?

Maybe it was because people often disliked Ferdinand. He was a loner, someone who kept his distance, a rough, gruff man who never seemed to laugh. Short and dark, he was unattractive to people. His looks didn't inspire trust. Those who didn't know him often failed to understand just how capable he was.

A less determined man might have given up. Not Ferdinand. He went to war again to prove his worth. But, in 1515, his soldiering came to an end. A lance wounded him in the knee. He walked with a limp for the rest of his life.

The future looked grim. Ferdinand was thirty-five years old, lame, and unpopular. People called him Clubfoot behind his back. There was only one thing for him to do—beg the king of Portugal himself to get him a ship and let him sail to Asia.

Chapter 3
A New King Listens

Lisbon, October, 1516. Ferdinand found that the city he once loved had become a lonely place. No one treated him like a war hero. His parents were long dead, and he had no wife or children. Aside from his religious faith, he felt like he had nothing. His best—possibly his only—friend was his slave.

Desperate, he went to King Manuel's court. But when Ferdinand kneeled before the king, Manuel announced that Ferdinand could move to another country for all he cared. "Serve whom you will, Clubfoot," the king said. "It is

King Manuel

a matter of indifference to us." It was a terrible insult. Still, this was the king. Tradition required that Ferdinand kiss the royal hand before leaving. As he tried to do so, the king swept his hand behind his back. Ferdinand, leaning forward on his bad leg, lost his balance and nearly fell.

Ferdinand's career in Portugal was finished. He understood that now. But if the king of his own country would not send him to sea, perhaps another king would—the king of Spain. Portugal's enemy was eager to win more of the spice trade.

One of its captains had just tried to find a sea route to Asia and had failed. This was Ferdinand's opening.

Ferdinand believed he knew a new way to get to the jewel of Asia—the Moluccas. He would sail southwest across the Atlantic and around the tip of the New World of the Americas. He would travel only through the Spanish half of the globe, not on any route that Portugal controlled. The trouble was that few people believed ships could sail west to the Moluccas. But Ferdinand did.

He knew that in 1513, the Spanish explorer Balboa had stood on a cliff on the west coast of South America. From there, Balboa had glimpsed a vast ocean that he'd named the South Sea. (We know it as the Pacific Ocean.) Plus, there were rumors of a strait—a thin body of water the

Vasco Núñez de Balboa

Spanish called *el paso*. Word had it that *el paso* ran through the bottom of South America, connecting the Atlantic to this South Sea. Based on maps and charts he'd seen, plus stories he'd been told, Ferdinand believed the Moluccas lay near the spot where *el paso* poured out into the sea.

No explorer had found the strait yet. Whoever did would claim the Moluccas for Spain, along with a trade route that other Spanish ships could follow. This man would get rich beyond his dreams. And he would make a fool of the Portuguese king.

Ferdinand got in touch with Diego Barbosa, a rich merchant who had also fled from Portugal for Spain. With his help, Ferdinand got a bishop,

a banker, and another merchant—all Spanish—to invest in his expedition. It was a start. But more money was needed. The only man rich enough to provide it was the Spanish king. Would he do it? No one knew. Charles I had just come to the throne. Only seventeen, he was still a boy, with no experience of power. And he was suspicious of anyone Portuguese.

But Ferdinand felt King Charles couldn't treat him any worse than King Manuel had. So in October, 1517, Ferdinand left Portugal forever and moved

King Charles I

Ferdinand and Beatriz

to Spain. There, he married Diego Barbosa's daughter, Beatriz. He was much older than she was. And she was much richer than he was.

Soon, Ferdinand found himself in the Spanish court. There, it didn't matter that he lacked charm. The king was looking for a daring captain with experience. No one was better qualified than Ferdinand. He impressed King Charles by showing him a special hand-painted leather globe and patiently tracing his route on it. Portugal, he insisted, wouldn't be able to interfere, since Ferdinand wouldn't be sailing through its waters. The Moluccas, he told the king, lay in Spanish territory.

GLOBES and MAPS

FOR HUNDREDS OF YEARS BEFORE THE TIME OF MAGELLAN, THE PEOPLE OF EUROPE BELIEVED THAT THE EARTH WAS FLAT. THEN, IN THE FIFTEENTH CENTURY, BRAVE EXPLORERS MADE MAPS AND CHARTS OF THE PLACES THEY VISITED. THEY BEGAN TO DISCOVER THE TRUE SIZE AND SHAPE OF THE EARTH.

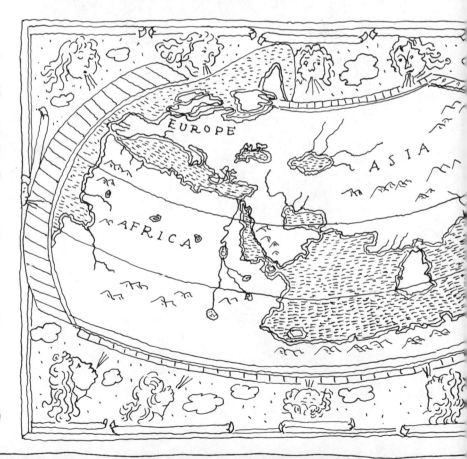

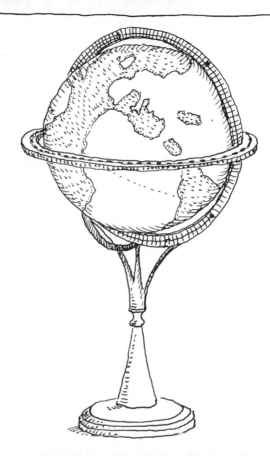

THE FIRST MAP SHOWING THE NEW WORLD WAS PUBLISHED IN 1507, AND THE FIRST SHOWING A ROUNDISH EARTH APPEARED IN 1508. MAGELLAN TOOK A HAND-PAINTED GLOBE MADE OUT OF LEATHER WITH HIM WHEN HE MET WITH THE KING OF SPAIN. THAT GLOBE HELPED TO CONVINCE THE KING TO FINANCE HIS VOYAGE. STILL, MANY OF MAGELLAN'S OWN MEN BELIEVED THEY WERE DOOMED TO SAIL RIGHT OVER THE EARTH'S EDGE.

The boy-king liked the dark, intense man from Portugal who spoke so passionately about his dream. In 1518 he agreed to make Ferdinand the captain-general of a voyage to the Moluccas. He'd pay for five ships to travel west, with enough supplies for a two-year trip. To make their deal official, he and Ferdinand signed a contract. It stated that Ferdinand would be governor of any island he discovered. He would be given two islands, if he found more than six. He would also get part of the profits from the voyage. If the expedition was a success, Ferdinand would become one of the richest, most powerful men in Europe.

Ferdinand had waited his whole life for this chance.

Chapter 4
Getting Ready

Now came the hardest time. Ferdinand couldn't set sail right away, as much as he wanted to. Five ships needed to be found, repaired, and then equipped with supplies. The crew had to be hired, along with the four captains who would sail under Ferdinand's command. He knew he must be patient, and prepare for anything. After all, there were no phones or radios, no rescue squads back then. In an emergency, he and his men would be on their own.

So he drew up a plan. First, he got the ships. The one called the *Trinidad* would be his. The other four—the *San Antonio*, the *Concepción*, the *Victoria*, and the *Santiago*—would be commanded by his captains.

All the ships were small. The largest was less than eighty feet—not even the distance from home plate to first base. But the biggest problem was their condition—they were secondhand and old. Their masts were shaky, their sails crumbling and torn. Plus, they were made of wood that had become so rotten, it seemed as if one big wave could sink all five ships.

Ferdinand had the ships repaired. Then he tried to find maps and charts to plan his exact route. But there were hardly any. He and his men would be the first Europeans heading to many of the places. Most of the time, the ships would be sailing blind.

Compass

Hourgla[ss]

As for tools to navigate, a compass would help Ferdinand determine direction. An hourglass would aid in telling time. Instruments called an astrolabe and a cross-staff could measure latitude—how far north or south from the equator the ship was. But there was no way to tell east from west. Longitude, which we use now, hadn't yet been discovered. Oftentimes, Ferdinand would just have to guess which way to go.

Cross-staff

Astrolab[e]

Then there was the food and drink needed for a long voyage. With no way to keep

anything cold, Ferdinand could take only food that took a long time to spoil. He bought cheese—21,120 pounds of it. And he got 570 pounds of pickled meat, 1,700 pounds of dried fish, 6,060 pounds of salt pork, 72,000 pounds of salt beef, and 200 barrels of sardines. There was more—1,512 pounds of honey, 3,200 pounds of raisins, 21,383 pounds of biscuits, 4,700 pounds of olive oil, 10,080 pounds of chickpeas, and 5,600 pounds of beans. He also got rice, lentils, onions, garlic, sugar, salt, flour, olives, figs, nuts, and wine. Everything was stored in barrels or baskets.

He also stocked up on tools, in case the ships needed to be fixed at sea. In addition, he bought

extra wood and rigging, canvas for new sails, barrels of tar, pieces of metal, and chunks of stone—replacement parts for anything that broke.

He didn't stop there. He prepared for battle too. If pirates, enemy ships, or unfriendly natives attacked, he wanted to be able to fight back. So, he armed

each ship with twelve cannons. Then he bought 6,000 pounds of gunpowder, 60 crossbows and 4,300 arrows, 1,000 lances, 120 short spears, 206 pikes, 1,140 darts, 200 shields, 100 suits of armor, 100 helmets, and 125 swords. Ferdinand was

Crossbow

ready for war. Even so, he didn't want to fight unless he had to. He packed gifts to give away or trade with native people. There were 1,000 mirrors, 600 scissors, 1,800

Lance and Shield

ARMOR

IN THE MIDDLE AGES, KNIGHTS (SOLDIERS) WORE SHIRTS MADE OF CHAIN LINKS, CALLED MAIL, TO PROTECT THEMSELVES IN BATTLE. THE PROBLEM WAS THAT MAIL DIDN'T STOP ARROWS, SPEARS, OR SOME SWORDS, SO THEY BEGAN TO WEAR METAL PLATES OF ARMOR. BY THE 1400S, THEY DRESSED IN FULL SUITS OF IT, FROM HEAD TO TOE. (POORER KNIGHTS SOMETIMES STOLE EXPENSIVE ARMOR OFF THE BODIES OF DEAD SOLDIERS.)

A FULL SUIT OF ARMOR WAS MADE UP OF MANY DIFFERENT PLATES AND WEIGHED AS MUCH AS SIXTY POUNDS. IT WAS HARD TO MOVE AROUND IN AND UNCOMFORTABLE, ESPECIALLY IN WARM WEATHER. AND BY THE LATE 1500S, AS GUNS AND CANNONS REPLACED SWORDS AND LANCES IN BATTLE, A SUIT OF ARMOR NO LONGER COULD PROTECT A SOLDIER.

skull

sight

visor

lance rest

breastplate

tasset

gauntlet

cuisse

poleyn

greave

sabaton

bells, 10,500 fishhooks, 4,800 knives, 550 pounds of glass beads, 1,500 combs, 4,000 bracelets, and more.

The hardest task of all was hiring the crew. Not many men wanted the job. After all, they had to sign up for two years and secretive Ferdinand refused to tell them where they were going. They wouldn't find out until they were already at sea. There was only one thing the sailors knew for sure—the trip would be dangerous. They could be taken prisoner or become shipwrecked. They might die of illness or drown.

But Ferdinand finally found 277 men willing to take a chance. Among them were criminals on the run, and men desperate for money. They were from all over the world—Portugal, Spain, Holland, Germany, Italy, France, Ireland, Greece, England, Asia, Africa, and more.

Most were deckhands, but some were highly skilled—carpenters, cooks, blacksmiths,

PIGAFETTA

FERDINAND ALSO AGREED TO BRING ALONG AN ITALIAN GENTLEMAN, ANTONIO PIGAFETTA. IT WAS A SMART MOVE. PIGAFETTA HAD NO SAILING SKILLS, BUT HE WAS AN EDUCATED MAN WITH A TALENT FOR LANGUAGES. WHEN THE SHIPS DOCKED IN FOREIGN LANDS, FERDINAND OFTEN SENT PIGAFETTA TO TALK TO THE NATIVES. PIGAFETTA SOON BECAME FERDINAND MAGELLAN'S BIGGEST FAN. AND THE REASON WHY HISTORIANS KNOW SO MUCH ABOUT WHAT HAPPENED ON FERDINAND'S VOYAGE IS BECAUSE PIGAFETTA KEPT A JOURNAL. IT SURVIVES TO THIS DAY.

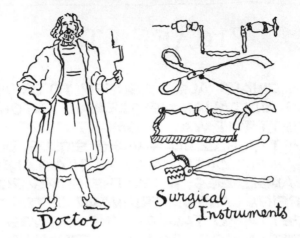

Doctor

Surgical Instruments

sail-makers, and boat pilots. There were also experienced officers as well as a doctor and a priest.

Finding captains was tricky. Ferdinand wanted to hire men he knew, Portuguese comrades he could trust. But two of the men in Spain who were putting up money for the trip did not like this idea. If Ferdinand's friends were captains, he would have too much power. In addition, they felt the king had promised Ferdinand more money than he deserved. So they decided to get rid of Ferdinand. They made Ferdinand hire three captains from Spain. These captains actually worked for them and planned to kill Ferdinand out at sea.

As if that wasn't bad enough, King Manuel of Portugal got word of Ferdinand's plans. He flew into a rage. The king never expected Ferdinand to succeed in Spain. Now that he had, the king accused Ferdinand of being a traitor. The king was going to do his utmost to make sure the voyage failed.

A year and a half passed before the ships were ready. At last, the moment Ferdinand had dreamt of since boyhood arrived. He was the captain-general of an expedition, and nothing else mattered. Not his young wife or newborn son. Not the danger of strange waters. Or King Manuel's threats. Ferdinand didn't even care that onboard, a nest of enemies surrounded him.

For across the seas lay wealth, fame, and glory. Ferdinand was sure of that.

Chapter 5
Tricky Seas

Tuesday, September 20, 1519. Ferdinand's five ships were about to start their great voyage. In a

port called San Lucar de Barrameda, near the great Spanish city of Seville, he and the crew of nearly three hundred men waved good-bye. Guns were fired, sails were raised. A hard-blowing wind shoved the ships out into the Atlantic. As they raced away, the men onboard thought of all the riches they hoped to discover. But their families were wondering if they'd ever see the men again.

The first stop was the Canary Islands, south of Spain. The instant he docked, Ferdinand received

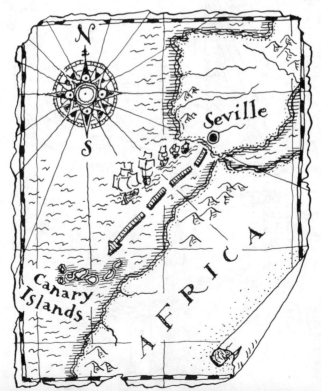

a secret message. Bad news! The three Spanish captains were plotting to kill him. That wasn't all— King Manuel of Portugal had sent ships to hunt him down.

Ferdinand had faced worse. He wasn't afraid. Instead of fighting right away, he used his brains. In order to confuse the Spanish captains, he pretended to agree with everything they said. To avoid enemy ships from Portugal, he gave orders to sail south along the African coast. It was a route no one would expect Ferdinand to take.

Ferdinand's ships headed for the equator through quiet seas. But a terrible storm arose near a country we now call Sierra Leone. Heavy rain pelted down. Lightning scorched the sky. Worst of all were the high winds, strong enough to blow the ships onto their sides.

The crew was terrified. Then the tops of the masts and the rigging seemed to catch fire. What was happening? Men wept and prayed. Like magic, the flames disappeared . . . then they came back, again and again. Yet nothing ever burned! At last, the crew realized they were watching Saint Elmo's fire. Today we know this is a bright glow caused by electricity in the air. To Ferdinand and his men, Saint Elmo's fire was a signal that the saint would protect them. No matter what, they would survive.

For two weeks, the storm raged. Then, at last, the waves died down. Ferdinand watched birds soar above him and fish fly through the air. But he dared not relax. He knew another kind of storm was brewing—one right onboard. One of the Spanish captains, Juan de Cartagena, was planning a mutiny—a rebellion at sea. But clever Ferdinand was not going to let that happen.

One day in November, he met with all his captains. Cartagena announced he would no longer obey orders. All Ferdinand did was raise his hand. It was a signal! The door burst open and armed sailors rushed to his side. They grabbed Cartagena, dragged him on deck, and threw him in irons. The other two Spanish captains realized that they had been outfoxed. Without a shot being fired, Ferdinand had foiled the mutiny.

Now he could enjoy the wonderful weather. The equator was near, and the air was warm. The men lay on deck, getting tan. The ships, soaked from the storm, dried out at last. Then everything went wrong.

The wind stopped completely. The sails lay flat all day and all night. They barely moved in a sea that seemed like mud. The sun beat down so hot that planks split and tar melted. Food spoiled, water ran short. Men fainted. Around the ships, sharks swam slowly, waiting to kill.

— The Doldrums —

The ships were in the Doldrums, a windless area of the Atlantic Ocean. For twenty days, not even the faintest breeze blew. The crew blamed Ferdinand. It was his orders that had brought them to this awful place. Perhaps the Spanish captains were right—they should mutiny. Ferdinand sensed the men's anger and kept to himself. For days, he saw no one. He was waiting, waiting for the wind.

SHIPS of the DAY

THERE WAS NOTHING SPECIAL ABOUT
FERDINAND'S SHIPS, EVEN THOUGH THEY
WERE TRAVELING THOUSANDS OF MILES
FROM HOME. LIKE ALL SHIPS OF THE TIME,
EACH ONE WAS MADE OF ROUGH WOODEN
PLANKS THAT DIDN'T FIT PERFECTLY
TOGETHER. TO PREVENT LEAKS, THE
SPACES BETWEEN THE PLANKS WERE
STUFFED WITH HEMP (WHAT ROPE IS
MADE OF) AND THEN COATED WITH TAR.
BUT SEAWATER ALWAYS MANAGED TO
SEEP IN, CONSTANTLY SLOSHING AROUND
THE HOLD (THE BOTTOM OF THE SHIP).
THE THREE MASTS, FROM WHICH THE SAILS
FLEW, WERE ALSO WOODEN. THERE WERE
NO ENGINES, SO IF THE WIND STOPPED OR
THE SAILS TORE OR THE MASTS FELL, THE
SHIPS COULD NOT MOVE.

mizzenmast

mainmast

crow's nest

foremast

poop deck

quarterdeck

foredeck

bowsprit

main deck

rudder

anchor cable

On the twenty-first day, tiny gusts of wind rippled the water. The gusts became a breeze. And the breeze filled out the sails. The ships began to move. At last, they were heading to South America. From there, the search for *el paso* would start.

Now there was no talk of mutiny. The crew looked forward to reaching land. For in those days, life on a ship was tough. Sailors had no privacy—they didn't even have rooms. They slept jammed together on deck. When it got dark, rats and

cockroaches crawled over their bodies. When it rained, the crew got drenched, as did all their belongings.

The deck wasn't just the bedroom—it was also the kitchen. Even though the ship was wooden,

meals were cooked on deck over an open fire. Since the wind sometimes blew hot ash and flames around, barrels of water stood nearby in case the ship started burning. Meals were served in shifts, without knives, forks, or spoons. The men used their hands to eat.

The toilet was awful. It was just a cage that hung off the back of the ship. If the waves were high, no one could reach it. Then the men used the bilge—where seawater leaks into the ship's hull, or bottom. Over time, the bilge became a sewer. The smell was so awful, it made them sick.

Still, the men did their work no matter how bad they felt. Otherwise, they had to answer to Ferdinand. They didn't like their captain-general, but they feared him. His dark hair and full black beard made him look as fierce as he was. A man of few words, he never shared his thoughts. He trusted only himself and his God.

On December 13, after nearly three months at sea, the ships reached Brazil. They were five thousand miles from Spain, in a gorgeous harbor near what is now Rio de Janeiro. All around them was the rain forest, with its wonderful smells. What pleasure to eat fresh food and drink from ice-cold streams!

Best of all, the men were outside Portuguese territory. There was no enemy to fear. The natives

N
Seville
Canary Islands
AFRICA
Tropic of Cancer
ATLANTIC
The Doldrums
Equator
BRAZIL
OCEAN
Tropic of Capricorn
Rio de Janeiro

of Brazil might have looked frightening with their tattoos, but they were friendly. They were happy to trade with the crew. One bell bought a basket of pineapples, one playing card five chickens. The crew even tried out the unusual beds— hammocks stretched between trees.

Brazil was like a vacation. But, right after Christmas, Ferdinand ordered the ships to sail south. It was time to find *el paso*.

Chapter 6
Frozen In

At first, it seemed easy. On January 11, 1520, Ferdinand spotted a wide opening in the coast. Was this the strait already?! His confidence soared.

But the opening was just a huge river in what we now call Uruguay. Cannibals were living there.

The crewmen were afraid. Talk of mutiny began again. The Spanish captains whispered that Ferdinand didn't know where *el paso* was. Best to sail east now, the old way to the Moluccas.

Ferdinand was furious. He wasn't about to give up the search. True, the strait was hard to find—but God would help him locate it. He declared it lay just a little farther south. Then he prayed silently that that was true.

On they sailed, the *Trinidad*, the *Victoria*, the *Concepción*, the *Santiago*, and the *San Antonio*. No European people had ever been this way before. February came, and a hint of winter cooled the warm air. In South America, winters last from April to September. Then, farther south, the weather became unusually cold. This wasn't just winter—they were approaching a frozen land.

Under a gray sky, icebergs jutted out of the water. Huge waves flung the five ships around and, below deck, leaks sprung everywhere. A bitter

wind tore sails and sometimes blew the ships
backwards. It was impossible to cook—the fires
on deck went out all the time. Hail and sleet and
then snow froze the men's clothes to their bodies.
Like the sails and rigging, their hair and beards
were coated with ice.

By March, they'd sailed a thousand awful miles. Today, we know the ships were near Antarctica, but back then no one had heard of such a place. The crew began to believe the captain-general was crazy. *El paso* was a fairy tale—it didn't exist.

But Ferdinand could think of nothing but the strait. He *had* to find it. No amount of protest

from the men could convince him to turn back. To show his determination, he joined them on deck, working harder than anyone, steering the ship himself. For weeks, he got just two hours of sleep a night. He never changed his clothes.

Six hundred miles later, there was still no strait.

Ferdinand realized the ships would have to wait out the winter in a safe harbor. On March 31, the ships rode thirty-foot waves into Port San Julian, a gray and rocky bay in what we now call Argentina. There were no people on its shores, only pudgy black-and-white birds that couldn't fly. Dark, sleek animals played in the water. Today, we know they were penguins and seals. But Ferdinand and his men had never seen creatures like them before.

The bay sheltered the ships from the wind and the waves. Still, the crew was uneasy. Where were they? They wanted to go home. Once again, the Spanish captains tried to mutiny. At midnight on April Fools' Day, thirty armed men seized the *San Antonio*. The *Victoria* fell next, and then the *Concepción*. Sailors loyal to Ferdinand were put in irons. It seemed as if the captain-general had finally lost his command.

But Ferdinand still had his *Trinidad*, and the loyal *Santiago*. Quick-witted and crafty, he came up with a plan. As the sun set and fog drifted in, six men rowed to the *Victoria*. They carried a letter for its rebel captain saying that Ferdinand was ready to make a deal. As the six boarded the ship, sixteen others snuck onto the *Victoria*. When the captain laughed off the letter, one of Ferdinand's men grabbed him and stabbed him to death. As the rebel captain's body was hung up for all to see, the crew of the *Victoria* surrendered. The ship was Ferdinand's once more.

The *Victoria* joined with Ferdinand's two ships to block the exit to the harbor. The *San Antonio*

and the *Concepción* were trapped—there was no way out. Ferdinand had outwitted the Spanish captains. The mutiny was over.

But Ferdinand wasn't finished. He wanted each sailor to know that disobedience meant death. So he had the *Victoria's* dead captain beheaded. The *Concepción's* captain met the same fate.

Then, forty-five mutineers were chained to one another by the ankles. For the rest of the winter, they were forced to do the hardest, dirtiest jobs. Juan de Cartagena's sentence was far worse. Ferdinand declared that he would be left behind in this icy wasteland.

Now Ferdinand and the crew got ready for winter. They hunted seals and wrapped themselves in the skins for warmth. In the few hours of daylight, they built huts and collected firewood. Ferdinand also had the men empty the ships, so repairs could be made. They needed to be in top shape when the search for *el paso* resumed.

That's when Ferdinand made a terrible discovery. Half his food and supplies were missing! They had been taken off the ships even before Ferdinand's expedition had left Spain.

Who was responsible?

King Manuel of Portugal, Ferdinand's longtime enemy.

Now, in this strange and icy land, where there was a storm every day, the captain-general and his men had to find food if they wanted to survive. They were lucky. There were ducks and birds to hunt, and crabs and fish in the water—enough to get them through the winter.

Months passed. Ferdinand and his men had only one another for company. Then, one day in June, a naked man appeared. Singing and dancing, he threw sand over his head. He was as tall as a

giant—Ferdinand only came up to his waist. But he was friendly, as were the others who soon appeared. Ferdinand named these people the Patagones, which means "big feet." Their land became known as Patagonia, and that is still its name today.

In August, it finally grew warm enough to leave. "We shall search for *el paso* until we find it," Ferdinand announced to the crew. But only four ships left the harbor on August 24. The fifth, the *Santiago*, had gone down in a storm a few weeks before.

A strong wind blew the *Trinidad*, the *Victoria*, the *Concepción*, and the *San Antonio* out to sea. As Ferdinand and the crewmen sailed away, Cartagena stood on shore.

He was never heard from again.

Chapter 7
The Pacific

The weather was foul on the open sea, so the expedition didn't get much farther. For the next two months, the ships had to drop anchor in a river. But, at last, the air lost its bite. The days grew so long that there were only three hours of darkness. On October 18, Ferdinand gave orders to set sail, and three days later the ships entered a blue-green bay. Above the rocky coast stood snow-capped mountains so high that clouds drifted around their peaks. They had come to a country we now call Chile.

To his captains, the beautiful bay seemed a dead end. But Ferdinand had a hunch. He ordered two of his ships, the *Concepción* and the *San Antonio*, to sail west to see where it led. But right after the two ships set out, a powerful storm struck. Wave after wave, some higher than the masts, smashed down. Ferdinand's own ship, the *Trinidad*, seemed about to go down. Crewmen on the *Victoria* were swept overboard. The *Concepción* and the *San Antonio* seemed to have disappeared. Had they sunk?

Two days passed. Ferdinand was in despair. To have come this far only to fail. Then, on the third day, a lookout suddenly started shouting. From the west raced two ships. The *Concepción* and the *San Antonio*!

To escape from the storm, they'd sailed from one bay into another, then another, like a chain . . . and they had discovered *el paso*!

Their discovery meant that there really was a

way to sail around the tip of South America. If the
expedition could make its way through the strait,
then it could keep heading west, west to the
Moluccas.

On all four ships, men cheered with joy. They danced, they hugged, they jumped up and down. And then they prayed. As cannons were fired, Ferdinand bowed his head and made the sign of the cross. He named *el paso* the Strait of All Saints. Now we call it the Strait of Magellan.

However, along with the good news came bad news. The men who found the strait reported that it was narrow and full of dead-end turns. The journey through it would be long and hard. If the ships took a wrong turn, they could be lost for weeks.

Ferdinand's captains told him it was best to stop now. The men were tired. Supplies were low. Claim the strait for the king of Spain, they advised. But don't go on.

Ferdinand refused. To him, it was madness not to continue. They would sail through the strait and reach the sea, he cried, "though we have nothing to eat but the leather wrapping from our masts."

So, into the strait they went, through the three bays. Granite walls a thousand feet high hemmed them in on both sides. They came to a fork— which way now? Ferdinand ordered the *Concepción* and

The Strait of Magellan

Pacific Ocean

Atlantic Ocean

the *San Antonio* to go one way. His *Trinidad* and the *Victoria* would go the other way.

A heavy mist lay over the captain-general's route. Thin rocks, sharp as nails, poked out of the water. Steering as carefully as possible, Ferdinand's ship and the *Victoria* sailed on for days. At last, pine mountains full of waterfalls came into view. Could the sea be close by?

Ferdinand sent out a scouting party. And, three days later, the scouts returned. They had reached the end of the strait! Ahead lay open water!

Ferdinand began to cry. He didn't care who saw his tears. *El paso* led to the sea. Across its waters lay the Moluccas. He had found the western route!

Back he sailed to share the news with the *Concepción* and the San Antonio. But only the *Concepción* was there. There had been a mutiny aboard the *San Antonio*, and she was heading back to Spain. The news hit Ferdinand hard. The *San Antonio* was his biggest ship. Even more importantly, she carried the most supplies. With the *San Antonio* gone, there wouldn't be enough food.

But Ferdinand would not accept defeat. He and the crew hunted and fished, and stocked up on food. Then they sailed for the sea past a place that blazed with light. It was as though a thousand fires were burning. He named the place Tierra del Fuego, "the land of fire." Today, we know the "fires" come from volcanoes.

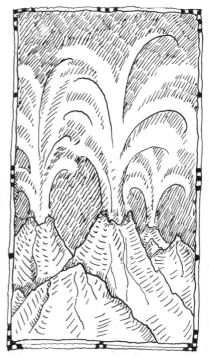

On November 28, the ships were plowing through rough waters. Then suddenly they were in an endless blue ocean. This must be the sea that Balboa had spied seven years before . . . the one he called the South Sea! It was so gentle; barely a ripple creased its surface.

Thirty-eight days had passed since the ships entered *el paso*. Now, 330 miles later, three ships had made it through. Surely, Ferdinand thought, the expedition wasn't more than three or four days away from the Moluccas.

Pacific Ocean

He had no idea how big this ocean was.

The men poured out on deck to pray. Ferdinand gazed at the water and shouted, "May the ocean be always as calm and benevolent as it is today. In this hope I name it *El Mar Pacifico*."

The Pacific. If Ferdinand had realized what lay ahead, he would have chosen a different name. He was about to cross the largest ocean on Earth, one that stretched across almost a third of the globe, its waters full of danger.

Chapter 8
The Crossing

All through December, Ferdinand expected to spy the Moluccas. He went north, then west. There was nothing but water. No land, no birds, only sharks. The night sky looked strange. Ferdinand didn't recognize the stars.

Six weeks passed. The sea was still calm, but onboard there was trouble. With little to do, the crew was bored and tempers were short. Fights broke out. Worse yet, supplies were running out.

Ferdinand grew gloomy. On January 20, 1521, he flew into a rage. Grabbing his charts, he flung them overboard. What good were they? He couldn't find the Moluccas. He was stuck in this never-ending sea.

Soon, all the remaining drinking water had turned yellow. It smelled so bad, the men held their noses while they drank. There was only enough for one sip a day.

Their solid food was going bad too. Biscuits crumbled into powder full of worms. The meat was so rotten, it glowed in the dark. Plus, there were long white maggots crawling through it. The men ate the food anyway, and when it ran out, they chewed wood chips, sawdust, and leather roasted over coals. Then they ate rats.

By this time, every member of the crew was sick. With no fresh fruit or vegetables, they had developed scurvy. Scurvy is an illness caused by lack of vitamin C. Their gums began to bleed, turn blue, and puff up. When the men tried to chew, their teeth fell out. Black circles shadowed their eyes. Sores covered their thin bodies. Their noses bled. Their elbows, knees, and ankles became swollen. A third of the crew was so weak, the men couldn't walk. One by one, they died and were buried at sea.

But Ferdinand didn't seem sick. Some historians think that he had a secret supply of fruit jam, rich in vitamin C. If he had this, why didn't he share it?

Was it just selfishness? Perhaps. Perhaps not. As captain-general, he needed to lead the expedition. And to do that, he had to stay healthy. In any case, Ferdinand knew he would die too, if more food wasn't found.

Then there was a miracle. On January 25, a small island came into sight. It had no trees or

fresh water, but there were fish, crabs, and birds. Plenty of food! When it rained, the men trapped the rainwater in barrels for fresh drinking water.

Once again, the ships set out to sea, hoping the Moluccas were close. But another six weeks passed. Again, they ran out of food. With the equator nearby, the sun scorched the decks. By now, twenty-nine men were dead, and most of the survivors could hardly move.

In early March, Ferdinand and his men ate the
last of the biscuit crumbs and sawdust. They
sipped the last of the water. If they didn't reach

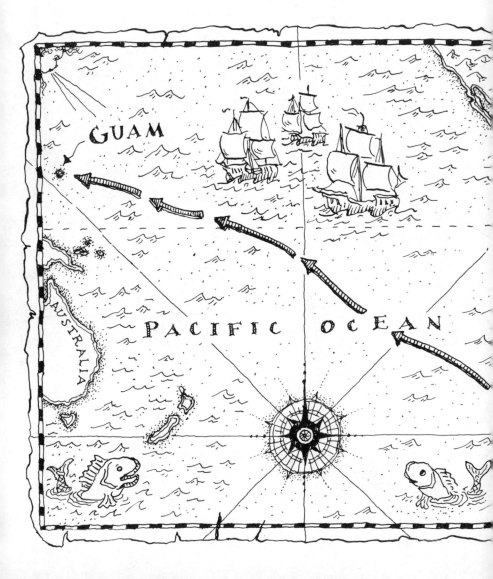

land soon, everyone would starve. In ninety-eight days, they'd sailed nine thousand miles, and they were more lost than ever. Only one man was still

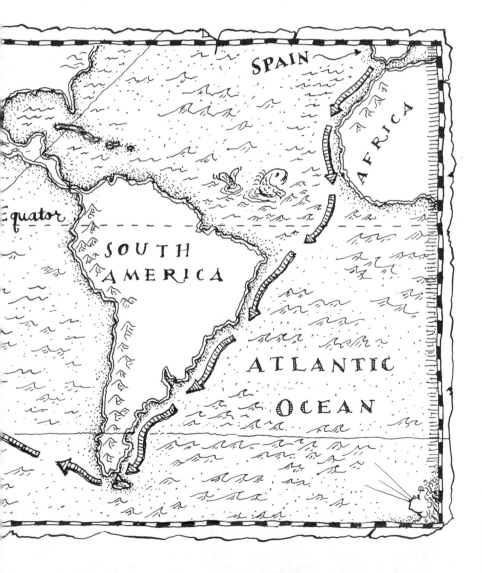

strong enough to climb to the lookout's post. When he got there, he couldn't believe what he saw. Out of the mist rose three islands with green mountains and waterfalls. "Praise God, land! Land! Land!" he cried. It was the country we now call Guam. The men dragged themselves to the railing—praying, crying, and hugging one another.

Chapter 9
The Last Battle

On and on the ships sailed, ever farther west. By the time they reached a group of islands that were part of today's Philippines, the expedition was seventeen thousand miles from home.

Ferdinand claimed the new islands for Spain. One was so rich in gold that every native wore a gold bracelet. The chief carried a dagger with a solid gold handle. And he had a gold-capped tooth.

Here was a chance to make a fortune! While the captain-general convinced the chief to trade with

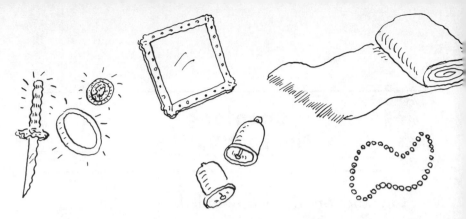

Spain, his men gave the natives mirrors, bells, and brightly-colored cloth in exchange for gold, pearls, and food.

Ferdinand wanted his share of riches too. But during the long, dangerous voyage, he had become convinced of something else as well. Something that he believed was more important than gold or spices. He believed that it was his duty to bring God and Christianity to the natives. He felt driven to save souls and preach about Jesus. On one island alone, he baptized twenty-two hundred people. Still, this didn't satisfy Ferdinand. He wanted everyone to recognize that his God was supreme.

One chief of an island refused to accept Ferdinand's religion. Nor did he accept the authority of the king of Spain. Ferdinand vowed to go to battle for his religion and his king. He was sure that if he did, God would protect him.

Was Ferdinand going mad? His officers begged him not to fight. But he told them, "I shall take with me none but volunteers. We shall see then whose trust is in God."

At midnight on April 27, Ferdinand and sixty men slipped into three boats. Dressed in armor, they began to row to the chief's island. Just as they were leaving, they heard a crow caw. It was a bad omen.

All night, they stayed in the boats, waiting for sunrise. But first light revealed a terrible sight.

There on the beach stood an army of fifteen hundred natives, ready to fight.

As always, Ferdinand had a plan. Eleven men stayed with the boats. He and forty-nine others jumped into the waist-deep water. Their heavy armor made wading ashore difficult. By the time they reached the beach, they were exhausted.

A spray of poison arrows greeted them, along with lances and stones. The weapons bounced harmlessly off their armor. But Ferdinand's men panicked anyway. There were native soldiers by the hundreds, fighting fiercely. When a poison arrow struck Ferdinand's leg, he was forced to order a retreat.

Scrambling into the water, his troops splashed to the boats. In their haste, they overturned one,

and fought one another to board the others. Hobbling from his wound, Ferdinand stayed on shore to give them cover. With eight loyal men, he held the native army back for an hour. It was his last stand. The native soldiers kept coming. They knocked off his helmet with stones.

Then a spear came out of nowhere and sliced into his face. Another cut his right arm so badly, he could no longer draw his sword. When he was speared in the left leg, he collapsed facedown in the surf. So many natives fell upon him that he disappeared from sight. One of his men later wrote, "And so they slew our mirror, our light, our comfort, and our true and only guide."

Ferdinand Magellan's body was never found.

Chapter 10
End of the Journey

On November 8, 1521, more than two years after leaving Spain, the *Trinidad* and the *Victoria* finally reached the Moluccas. Three months later, the *Victoria* sailed home to Spain, loaded down with spices. The ship arrived, a ghost of herself, on

September 6, 1522. After twenty-seven thousand miles, she was rotted through and leaking. Just eighteen of her crew were still alive. Even so, nobody in Spain expected anyone to return. Long

ago, everyone on Ferdinand's expedition had been given up for dead. Yet the few survivors had accomplished what Ferdinand Magellan set out to do. They had sailed around the world.

The men were greeted as heroes. King Charles invited them to his palace. But the spices they brought home earned only enough money to cover the expenses of the trip. For all the hope of riches that sent Ferdinand Magellan to sea, no profit was made from his voyage.

The *Trinidad* left the Moluccas in April, 1522. But, after three months at sea, with the crew dying from scurvy, the ship returned to the islands. It was not until 1525 that the *Trinidad*—with only four survivors—finally reached Spain.

And the captain-general, Ferdinand Magellan? He was a forgotten man. His wife and child were dead. He had died halfway through the journey. Most of his men spoke poorly of him, when they mentioned him at all.

The expedition was considered a failure. The long, difficult route had made no money for traders. Other captains who set out on the same route as Magellan couldn't even find Ferdinand's strait. King Charles of Spain eventually sold the rights to the Moluccas to Portugal. The long voyage seemed to have accomplished very little.

Of course, it had accomplished a lot. Now, people knew that the world was much larger than had been thought. For the first time, there was

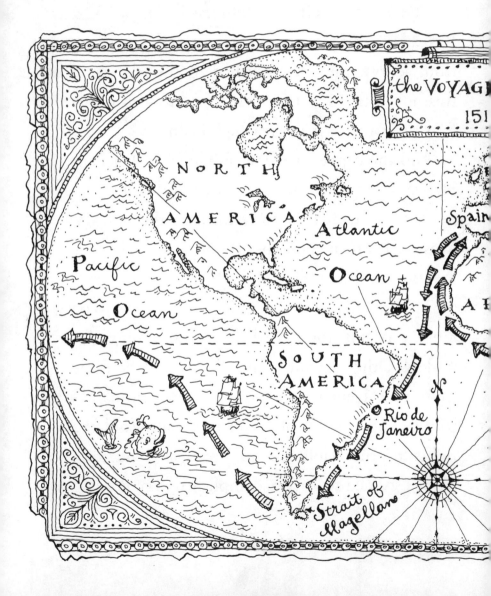

proof that the Pacific and Atlantic oceans were
connected. And there was absolute proof that the
Earth was round . . . round and covered with so

much water that circling it in a ship was possible.

As the years passed, people came to realize how daring Ferdinand Magellan's voyage had been. This fierce little man had changed what they knew about the world. A new age of exploration began, with voyages all over the Pacific Ocean. Maps were redrawn and globes came into use. The great civilizations of Europe, Asia, and the Pacific were brought closer.

Ferdinand had started it all. Today, Ferdinand Magellan is famous for being a great seaman, a brilliant navigator, and a bold explorer. He was also a murderer and an intolerant man. His religious beliefs had to be everyone else's beliefs. But his actions were typical of his time. Ferdinand Magellan sailed thousands of miles only to die without purpose on a strange beach. Yet, though he didn't complete his journey, he is recognized, and rightly so, as the first man to sail around the world.

FERDINAND MAGELLAN

Timeline of Magellan's Life

1480	Ferdinand is probably born
1492	Ferdinand is appointed Queen Leonora's page
1496	Ferdinand becomes a government clerk and helps set up expeditions
1505	Ferdinand goes to war against the Arabs
1509	Ferdinand is wounded for the first time
1510	Ferdinand tries to return to Portugal, but is shipwrecked
1512	Ferdinand may have sailed to the Philippines for the first time
1515	Ferdinand is wounded for the second time, and now has a permanent limp
1516	The Portuguese king refuses to send Ferdinand on an expedition
1517	Ferdinand leaves Portugal forever and moves to Spain
1518	The Spanish king agrees to finance Ferdinand's voyage west to the Moluccas
1519	Ferdinand and his men leave to find *el paso*—the western passage to the Moluccas
1520	Ferdinand foils a mutiny, spends the winter near Antarctica, and names Patagonia
1520	Ferdinand finds *el paso* and names the Pacific Ocean
1521	Ferdinand claims the Philippines for Spain, and dies in battle
1522	Ferdinand's ship, the *Victoria*, reaches Spain, the first circumnavigation of the world

TIMELINE OF THE WORLD

Bartolomeu Dias of Portugal is the first European to round the Cape of Good Hope, the southern tip of Africa	1488
Columbus is the first European to discover the New World	1492
The Treaty of Tordesillas is signed, dividing the world between Spain and Portugal	1494
Vasco da Gama of Portugal finds a sea route to India	1498
John Cabot of England explores the east coast of North America	1498
The Portuguese claim Brazil	1500
Amerigo Vespucci of Portugal explores what is now South America	1501
The New World is named "America"	1507
Balboa is the first European to see the Pacific Ocean, which he calls the South Sea	1513
Juan Ponce de León of Spain explores Florida	1513
Portuguese traders reach China	1520
Ferdinand Magellan is the first to sail the Pacific	1521
Hernando Cortés of Spain conquers the Aztecs in Mexico	1521
Magellan's men complete the first circumnavigation of the world	1522
Francisco Pizarro of Spain conquers Peru	1531
Jacques Cartier of France reaches Quebec in Canada	1541
Hernando De Soto of Spain sails the Mississippi River	1541
The Portuguese are the first Europeans to reach Japan	1542
Sir Francis Drake of England completes the second circumnavigation of the globe	1580

BIBLIOGRAPHY

Fritz, Jean. **Around the World in a Hundred Years: From Henry the Navigator to Magellan.** G.P. Putnam's Sons, New York, 1994.

Hargrove, Jim. **Ferdinand Magellan.** Children's Press, New York, 1991.

Jacobs, William Jay. **Magellan: Voyager with a Dream.** Franklin Watts, New York, 1994.

Lauber, Patricia. **How We Learned the Earth Is Round.** Harper and Row, New York, 1992.

Levinson, Nancy Smiler. **Magellan and the First Voyage Around the World.** Clarion Books, New York, 2001.

Macdonald, Fiona. **Magellan: A Voyage Around the World.** Franklin Watts, New York, 1998.

Maestro, Betsy and Giulio. **The Discovery of the Americas.** Lothrop, Lee & Shepard, New York, 1990.